D0847224

WITHDRAWN

# Homes in Cold Places

**Alan James**

Lerner Publications Company
Minneapolis

All words printed in **bold** are explained in the glossary on page 30.

*The author wishes to dedicate this book to Joan and John Todd.*

Cover illustration *A Lapp boy and his mother outside their laavu home.*

First published in the U.S. in 1989 by Lerner Publications Company.

First published in 1987 by Wayland (Publishers) Ltd.

**Library of Congress Cataloging-in-Publication Data**

James, Alan, 1943-
Homes in cold places / Alan James.
p. cm.
Bibliography: p.
Includes index.
Summary: Describes how homes in cold climates are designed and constructed.
ISBN 0-8225-2131-8 (lib. bdg.)
1. Architecture, Domestic—Cold regions—Juvenile literature. 2. Vernacular architecture—Cold regions—Juvenile literature. [1. Architecture. Domestic—Cold regions. 2. Dwellings.]
I. Title.
NA7117.C64J36 1989 88-22930
728—dc19 CIP
AC

Printed in Italy by G. Canale & C.S.p.A.,—Turin
Bound in the United States of America

1 2 3 4 5 6 7 8 9 10 97 96 95 94 93 92 91 90 89

# Contents


What is a cold place? . . . . . . . . . . . 4

Homes in cold places . . . . . . . . . . . 6

Keeping warm . . . . . . . . . . . . . . . . 8

Saving heat . . . . . . . . . . . . . . . . . . . 10

Building materials . . . . . . . . . . . . 12

More building materials . . . . . . . 14

Building skills . . . . . . . . . . . . . . . . 16

Design . . . . . . . . . . . . . . . . . . . . . 18

Space and shape . . . . . . . . . . . . . 20

Living habits . . . . . . . . . . . . . . . . 22

Family groups . . . . . . . . . . . . . . . 24

Changing cultures . . . . . . . . . . . . 26

Comfort in the home . . . . . . . . . . 28

Glossary . . . . . . . . . . . . . . . . . . . 30

Books to read . . . . . . . . . . . . . . . 31

Index . . . . . . . . . . . . . . . . . . . . . . 32

# What is a cold place?

The very cold parts of the world are mostly in the far north and far south. Cold expanses of ice cover the north polar (Arctic) and south polar (Antarctic) regions.

The Antarctic has very cold winters and **temperatures** can fall to -76°F (-60°C) or lower. The temperature at the South Pole is always well below the **freezing point.** The North Pole is somewhat warmer, and the temperature there may rise above the freezing point on occasions. But the Arctic often has temperatures as low as -22°F (-30°C) even in the summer sunshine.

The North and South poles are often very windy with snowstorms and "**whiteout**" conditions. In polar regions, six months of darkness in winter are followed by six months of daylight in summer.

The ice in the Antarctic is more than 2½ miles (4 kilometers) thick in places. There is little plant life, but there are polar bears, fish, seals, and walrus in the Arctic and penguins and fish in the Antarctic.

**Tundra lands** have short summers, when the temperature rises above

***Left*** *A polar bear and her cubs in the Arctic*

***Right*** *Map of the world showing the different climates*

freezing, and moss, grass, and low shrubs can grow. But in polar lands there is constant cold. The Arctic Sea is frozen for most of the year. In winter, the sea might freeze to a depth of 6 feet (2 meters).

The cold places of the world include Iceland, Greenland, Alaska, northern Canada, northern U.S.S.R., the Antarctic land mass, the tip of South America, and some islands such as the Falklands in the southern Atlantic and Spitzbergen in the Arctic Sea. The northern parts of Norway, Sweden, and Finland also have very cold winters.

Temperatures can become very low in regions that are high above sea level, such as the Alps in Austria and Switzerland and the Himalayan Mountains in India and Tibet. There are also cold places in the **tropics.** In the mountains of Peru and western Mexico it is bitterly cold in winter.

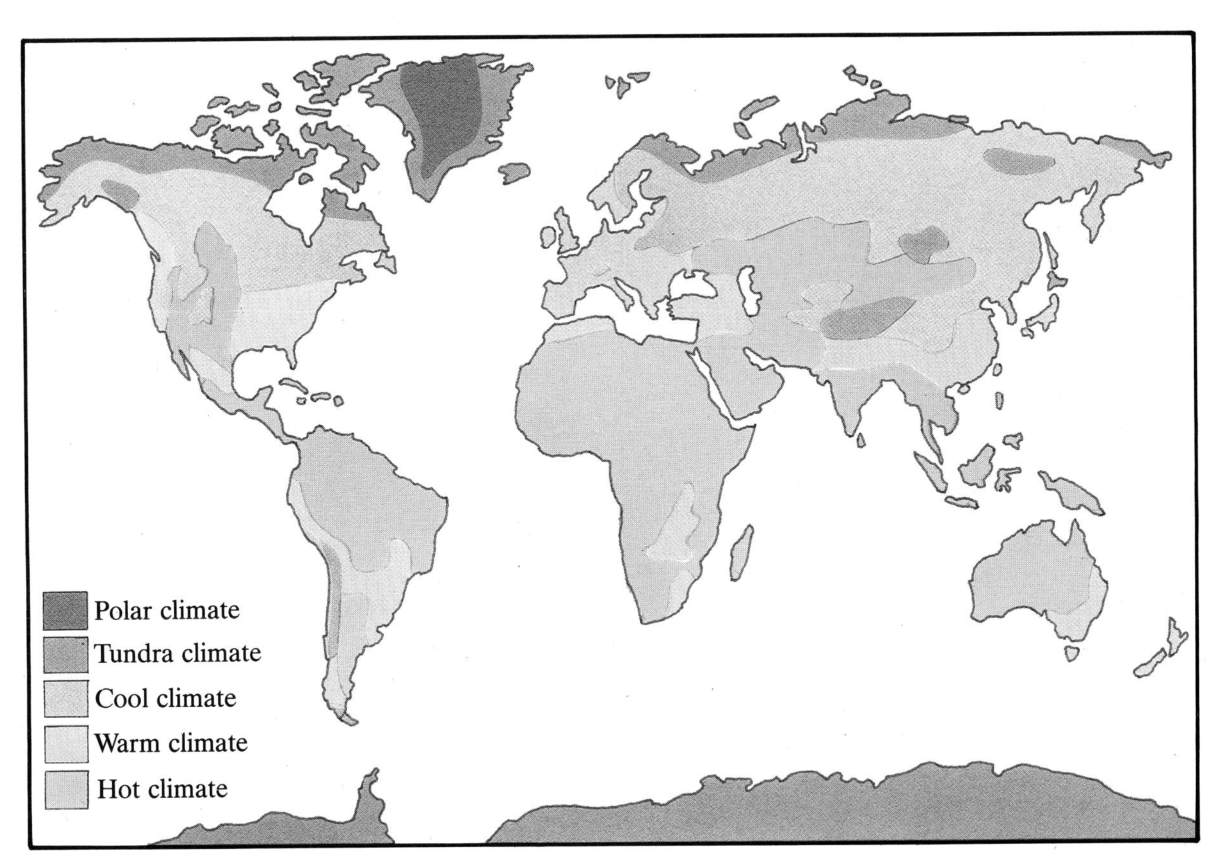

# Homes in cold places

People who make their homes in extremely cold places face very special problems. Few people live in the very coldest parts of the earth. Because of the icy conditions which exist for most of the year, these places are difficult to reach and to supply with food and materials. No one lives permanently in the Antarctic. Human settlement is limited to camps of **research** scientists, and military bases that are set up by certain countries.

People need homes that protect them from the cold temperatures and icy winds in the most efficient way possible. They must use building materials that they can obtain fairly easily. Once a home has been warmed by fuel, it must be able to hold in the heat. The cold **climate** helps people decide what kinds of houses to construct. People use many different building materials and shapes to protect themselves from cold weather.

One of the most important stages

*Right* Homes that are built of wood need to be well protected from the cold. This house is in New Jersey, which has very cold winters.

*Left* One settlement in the Antarctic is this research base in Signey, South Orkney.

of building a home is laying a firm **foundation** in the ground, on which the home can stand safely. In the tundra, the topsoil is frozen solid for nine months of every year. The soil lower down, called the **permafrost,** is always frozen and water cannot drain through it. Often, the topsoil becomes very damp or even waterlogged in the summer when the ground thaws and water cannot drain through the permafrost. When this happens, houses can become lopsided and damaged because the topsoil cannot provide stability for their foundations.

Modern Canadian homes also face this problem of frozen ground, although to a lesser extent. Foundations are laid below the level that the frost reaches in winter so that buildings remain stable as the earth freezes and thaws. Because of this, every Canadian home has a basement below ground that provides storage room or a play area.

# Keeping warm

In cold places, the sun's heat does not raise the temperature to a level that is comfortable for humans. In these places, houses are built to provide warm conditions for people indoors. A house is able to store overnight some of the heat collected from the sun during the day.

However, the heat from the sun is not enough to make a house comfortable in cold climates. The home has to be heated in other ways to make the temperature inside higher than the temperature outside. Since bodies give off heat, simply putting people or animals into a house is one way of making the house a little warmer.

***Below*** *An Inuit needs a long knife to cut snow blocks, fur clothing, and lamps for light and heat in the igloo.*

Another way to warm a house is to use electricity to heat radiators and electric heaters. A small amount of heat comes from stoves, electric lights, and electrical gadgets. Houses are also heated by furnaces fueled by coal, gas, wood, or oil.

A comfortable temperature in a house is at least 66°F (19°C) for someone at rest and slightly less for someone who is moving about and using **energy**. The warmth and the amount of clothing people wear affect their comfort.

Wearing a lot of clothing helps to **insulate** the body from the cold. In the same way, a house can be kept warmer through insulation which **conserves** whatever heat is generated within the house.

***Below*** *Inside this Canadian Arctic trading post there is a central stove. The post trades in furs and leather goods.*

# Saving heat

The amount of heat a house can store depends on the building materials used. A brick building, for instance, is able to retain a great deal of heat. Cement, used increasingly in buildings today, also retains heat.

No matter what material is used to build a house, much of the heat that is used to keep the house warm escapes to the outside. No building material can stop heat from going through it. When the outside is colder than the inside of a house, there will always be a flow of heat to the outside—through walls, windows, the

*Most heat is lost from a home through the walls, the roof, and the windows. Here are some of the ways a house can be insulated to reduce this heat loss.*

roof, the floor, and through drafty gaps.

A less sturdy home—such as a wooden building—allows heat to escape fairly quickly through the walls and the roof. However, such a home can be warmed more rapidly than a brick home.

A house can be insulated against the cold to help keep in much more heat. **Drafts** from windows and doors can be stopped by applying **caulking.**

Thick, heat-retaining rolls of **fiberglass insulation** serve as attic insulation and stop heat from escaping through the roof. Insulating materials can also be injected into **wall cavities** to reduce heat loss through outside walls.

Wall-to-wall carpets help stop heat from getting out through the floor. Wood floors need to be specially insulated to stop heat from going into the ground. **Double** or **triple glazing** stops some heat from escaping through windows and also stops drafts. Wooden window frames give better insulation than metal frames.

Older kinds of houses were also built to keep heat inside. Old wooden houses in Scandinavia sometimes had **sod** roofs. Today, in Iceland, houses are still being built with sod roofs as a cheap, efficient way of saving heat.

Snow **igloos** were used by Eskimos (or Inuit) as temporary homes when they were hunting. Igloos had only one door and furs lining the floor helped provide insulation. Today, modern Inuit often live in wooden homes insulated with fiberglass insulation.

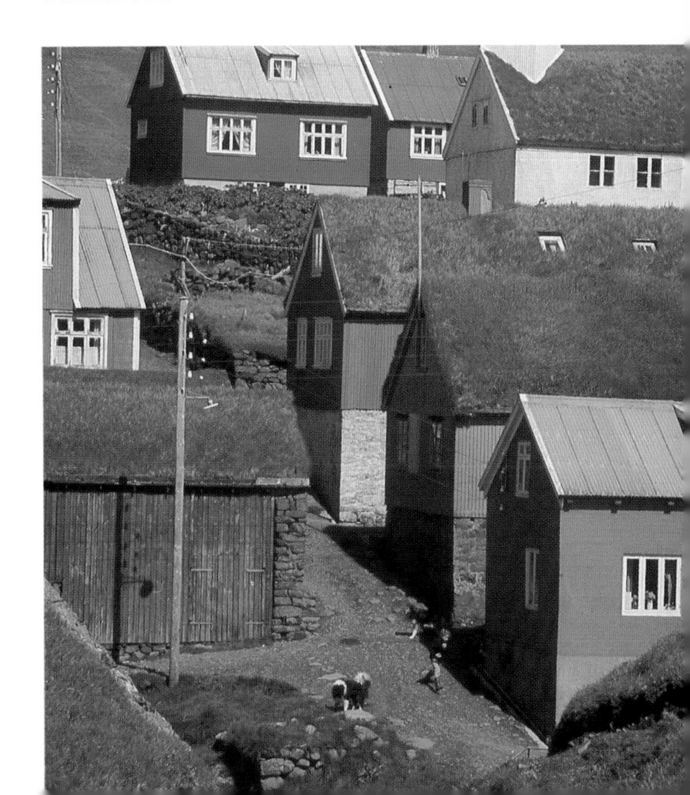

***Right*** *Putting sod on the roofs of these houses in the Faroe Islands is an old method of insulating against heat loss.*

# Building materials

People use the building materials that they know how to handle and that are available to them. Homes are built with timber, bricks, snow, and concrete.

The Inuit people made igloos from many materials including snow, logs, and earth. Some were made of stones and sod. Others were made of caribou skin and sod with a frame of wooden poles or whalebones. Some igloos were built partly underground and were kept warm and well-insulated by the earth. Often, only a lamp was needed to keep the igloo warm.

An Inuit can build a snow igloo in about an hour. The builder uses a knife to cut blocks of snow, making sure to use firm snow so that the blocks don't crack. He or she places the blocks in a wide **spiral** that leans slightly inward. The blocks come together on top to create a dome. A large igloo may have a window made of a piece of freshwater ice.

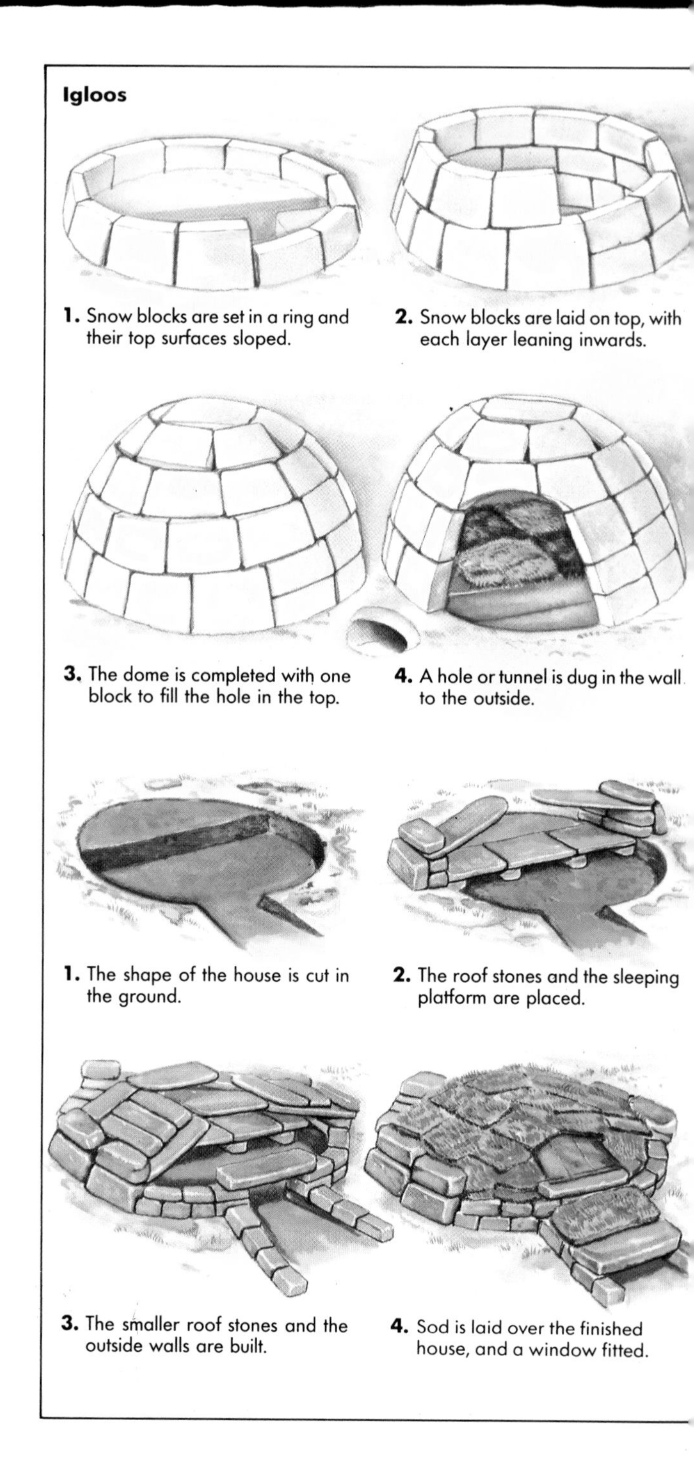


***Right*** *Methods of building two kinds of igloos. One is made with snow, the other with stones and sod.*

An igloo sometimes has a long, low entrance tunnel and three inside chambers set in a row. Thick, fur curtains hung between the chambers create an **airlock** between the inner room of the igloo and the cold outdoor air.

Heat from lamps and from bodies raises the temperature inside the igloo. This melts a little of the snow and seals the joints between the blocks with a thin layer of ice. A small hole is made in the roof to release heat and to prevent the snow from melting too much.

Another airtight construction is the **yurt**, built by Mongolian **nomads**. A thick felt covering made from pressed animal hair is laid over a **lattice** framework to form a round tent. Extra layers of felt are added in winter.

***Left*** *The first stage in building a yurt, the home of Mongolian nomads. A lattice framework is placed in a circle to form the structure of the tent.*

***Right*** *The finished yurt has a thick covering of felt or pressed animal hair, laid over the wooden framework.*

# More building materials

Permanent homes in cold places are built with materials such as wood, brick, stone, and concrete.

Wooden houses need less heat to warm them up than do stone, brick, and cement houses. Wooden houses need to be carefully insulated to stop that heat from escaping.

A chalet is a wooden house found in the mountains of Austria, Switzerland, Germany, and France. Chalets are square and are made from heavy wooden planks. The ground floor might have a low ceiling and can be used as a storage space, a barn, or a cattle shed.

Roofs on chalets are covered with wooden **shingles**, **slate**, or stone slabs. In very exposed, windy areas, planks and even heavy stones might be used to keep the roof from blowing off when it is stormy!

People also build permanent homes with brick and stone. Bricks are made from clay baked at high temperatures. Clay is also used to make pipes and roofing tiles. Stone is cut from a quarry. Brick and stone walls are sealed with mortar, which is a mixture of sand, cement, and water.

Concrete is made of gravel (very small stones), sand, and cement. When it is mixed with water it makes

***Left*** *This wooden chalet near Bern, Switzerland, is typical of the attractive houses in the Swiss valley villages.*

***Left*** *The roof of this chalet in Switzerland might be covered with shingles, slate, or stone slabs as protection against the snow.*

***Below*** *Homes built close to each other, such as these apartments in Murmansk, U.S.S.R., help conserve heat.*

a stiff paste that hardens in a few hours. The mixture can be poured around steel rods that strengthen the hardened concrete.

Today, wood, brick, stone, and concrete are used to build houses throughout the world. It is often expensive to transport these materials to cold, normally **inaccessible** places. But houses that are made of these materials and have good insulation and heating systems provide excellent shelter from cold weather.

# Building skills

The sorts of homes people build depend on their building skills and the materials that are available. They might make simple homes or more complex ones. Many different building skills are needed to construct homes in cold areas.

Settlers in North America once built log houses because they were simple to make and also provided shelter against the weather and against attack by enemies. To make a log house, settlers chopped down trees and trimmed them with an axe. They placed these logs on top of each other to form walls and filled in the cracks with mud, moss, or

***Above*** *A Lapp might live in a laavu, a tent made of sticks and reindeer skin, as a temporary home when traveling.*

***Left*** *Building a log cabin in Finland*

clay. The roof was made of heavy planks of wood.

The floor of the house might simply be packed earth. But sometimes split logs with the flat sides upward formed a floor with a straight walking surface. Doors and window **shutters** hung from wooden pegs or leather hinges.

Nomadic peoples often build tents because they are simple to build and easy to transport. The Mongolian peoples of the U.S.S.R. and the Lapp peoples of northern Scandinavia use tents when they travel. A Lapp **laavu** is built by covering a central frame of sticks with canvas or reindeer skins.

Many homes, such as the tall apartment houses in northern Canada and the U.S.S.R., are more difficult to build. Some of these modern houses are **prefabricated** or partly built before they arrive at the building site. The parts are easily assembled on the site. This method of building is useful in cold climates because houses can be assembled quickly during the short season in which it is warm enough to build. Building methods and materials are improving all over the world as people make great strides forward in technology.

***Left*** *The walls of a prefabricated house can quickly be fixed into position. This is an advantage in cold places where there is a short building season.*

# Design

The way a house is designed (planned and laid out) depends on the needs and lifestyle of the people who will live in it. The cold climate also has a big effect on the way a house is designed.

In cold places, houses are designed so that they will keep in as much heat as possible. For this reason, many houses have outer walls with a fairly small **surface area.** A great deal of heat can escape through walls and the roof, so a small outer surface helps to reduce the heat loss. Dome-shaped structures, such as snow igloos, have relatively small outer surfaces. A dome is the ideal shape for a cold weather house because it allows the greatest amount of space to be used inside the building, while it exposes the smallest area outside.

In cold places in the northern half of the world, buildings can collect some energy from the sun if the houses are long and if the largest windows face south. In the southern half of the world where the sun shines strongest from the north, north-facing windows can help a house collect energy from the sun. But many homes in cold places are not designed to benefit much from the sun.

In Sweden and parts of Canada, however, some houses have solar panels on the roof. The panels take solar energy from sunlight and turn it into heat energy which can be used to heat water.

At Byrd Station and the Amundsen-Scott Station in Antarctica, networks

***Left*** *Houses at Baker Lake in Canada have been built in the same shape as an igloo. The shape is ideal because it provides a large space inside, while a relatively small area is exposed to the cold outside.*

***Left*** *Some homes in cold places can benefit from the sun by catching solar energy on a rotating panel and converting it to heat energy.*

of tunnels have been designed to connect living quarters with laboratories and workshops. Because of these tunnels, researchers at the stations do not have to face the bitterly cold weather and freezing winds when they walk from building to building.

***Right*** *Densely packed apartments behind the Moskva River in Moscow*

# Space and shape

The design and shape of a house depend on the climate of a particular place. For instance, houses in cold countries often have small rooms with low ceilings, so that they can be heated fairly quickly. People's habits, needs, and customs also influence their house designs.

The Huichol, Native American people who live in the mountains of western Mexico, face bitterly cold winters. Their homes are made from stone and adobe (mud) bricks and have **thatched roofs.** The Huichol have different huts for different purposes, such as eating and sleeping. Each hut can be heated as it is needed.

***Above*** *This Inuit family from the Canadian Arctic lives in a wooden home insulated with fiberglass insulation to keep it warm.*

On the extreme southern tip of South America at Tierra del Fuego, some people build simple shelters made from animal skins. The skins are fastened to trees on one end and then tied to branches hammered into the ground. These shelters give protection from extremely cold winds and heavy storms from the sea.

In northern Scandinavia, some Lapps still use tents when herding reindeer. A large summer tent is used by the whole family. Inside, a central fire provides heat for comfort and cooking.

Rooms in log cabins are often rectangular or square. These are the simplest shapes to make from long lengths of thick lumber. The building heats up quickly when a fire or stove is lit.

The earth can provide insulation and help keep a house warm. Igloos were built partly underground to take advantage of this insulation. In some cold places, modern **earth-sheltered houses** are built partly underground and are kept well insulated by the earth.

***Left*** *The Quechua, native people of the Andean Highlands, make their homes in adobe huts. Some huts have roofs of thick pampas grass.*

***Below*** *A Lapp encampment with several laavu tents on Norway's north shore*

# Living habits

People lead varied lives in the cold places of the world. Some people are settled and stay in one place, perhaps in the same village or town, for all of their lives. Their homes are permanent ones, made of brick, stone, concrete, or wood.

Other people travel seasonally, such as the Inuit when hunting seals, or the Lapps when following their reindeer. These wanderers are called nomads because they travel from place to place. They often live in light tents. Today, Lapps often use a one-story, wooden home as a permanent base. But those Lapps that still follow reindeer in winter make camps and sleep in small tents on the snow.

More and more, Inuit people live settled lives in wooden homes built by their governments. Some Inuit still use traditional building skills and make igloos with snow and animal skins when they go hunting. The Inuit of Greenland live in a more traditional way than those of northern Canada. They have formed organizations to try to protect their traditional lifestyle.

At the research bases in Antarctica, people often do not go outdoors throughout the long winter. They sometimes have to wait a long time for mail and supplies to arrive, because the weather and frozen conditions prevent ships and airplanes from reaching them regularly.

***Left*** *This house, built by the Inuit in the mountains of Alaska, is made of mud and grass.*

***Left*** *Winters in the Himalayan Mountains are very severe. These stone buildings on steep slopes provide permanent homes for people in Ladakh, India.*

***Right*** *An Inuit family outside their wooden home on St. Lawrence Island, Alaska*

# Family groups

The size of a house depends on such things as income (how much money you earn), habit, **culture**, and the number of people who will be living inside the house. Most homes in cold places are designed for one family, although in many countries three and sometimes four generations of a family all live together in one house. Children might have great-grandparents, grandparents, and parents living in the house with them. This kind of family grouping is found in villages in the U.S.S.R. and Tibet. In large cities in the U.S.S.R., Canada, and Europe, people often move away from their relatives to find work in new places.

People living in small settlements in the Arctic might live a long distance from any of their relatives. A small town in northern Canada often consists of a wooden house for each family, a government office, a store, a church, an electricity generating plant, a garage, a school, a clinic, and an office of the Royal Canadian Mounted Police.

A few families live in the Antarctic. They are the families of research scientists or soldiers established at the bases there.

A country's culture influences how many children are in each family.

***Left*** *This remote town in the Canadian Arctic contains all the essential facilities, but its residents may live a long distance from their relatives.*

One benefit of a bigger family is that it means a warmer house, and this is important in some cold places. Each person produces heat just by being alive. Children produce about half the heat of adults. A sleeping or sitting adult produces about the same heat as a 60-watt electric light bulb. An adult doing light work produces 150 watts of heat, and a person doing heavy, strenuous work produces 500 watts of heat.

***Above*** *In the U.S.S.R., large family groupings are more usual in the villages than in the cities. Here several generations of a large Tajik family are seated on the floor for a meal.*

# Changing cultures

People can choose to build homes of many different types, styles, and sizes. In cold places, a house may be built in a lonely outpost, in a clustered group settlement, or among many other houses in a large city. In Siberia, U.S.S.R., old wooden houses, built long ago, can still be seen in some villages. Many of these homes have attractive carved decorations around doors and windows. These decorations show traditional patterns and styles that are unique to the culture of this region.

But building methods, materials, and designs are changing in many cold places. Modern house designs and methods of constructing large houses are becoming very similar in all parts of the world. Today there are even metal igloos that can be moved when people move to a new place.

Recently, oil, copper, uranium, and gas have been discovered in the Arctic, deep under the ground. More scientists and technicians are now living in towns and settlements in this remote region. Machines and materials have to be transported there, and **industrial** changes are taking place as the Arctic slowly becomes a more developed area.

No single country owns Antarctica. Britain, France, Chile, Argentina, and New Zealand are some of the countries that claim part of Antarctica for themselves. But the U.S.A., the U.S.S.R., and other countries do not accept these claims. Some countries, such as West Germany, China, India, and Brazil, have settlements in Antarctica all year long.

Scientists and explorers work in Antarctica. They are there to find out more about freezing conditions. They drill through deep ice to find out about the climate of the past. They can measure how thick the ice is by bouncing radio signals off the ice from an airplane.

*Left* — *An old wooden house in Siberia, U.S.S.R., with traditional decorations around the windows*

***Right*** *A modern igloo used as a hunter's hut in Greenland*

***Below*** *Exploring the waters of the Antarctic in a rubber dinghy*

# Comfort in the home

All people need some private space, where they can keep their belongings and feel safe and secure. A home provides this security. The standard of comfort it provides can vary a great deal from one house to another. The comfort of homes in cold places depends on several things. These include the severity of the climate in a particular place, whether the house is temporary or permanent, and the building materials and skills that are available there. Comfort also depends on the type of heating and the kinds of insulation that are used to keep the house warm and dry.

Today, many permanent homes have central heating systems that generate heat from one place and send it to radiators or ducts placed throughout the house. Some homes are warmed by stoves. Many people still like to burn wood or coal in the fireplace, because it makes a room cozier.

In parts of Scandinavia, such as Finland and Sweden, people build rooms called saunas in which they can relax and get clean at the same time. The sauna is filled with hot steam which makes a person sweat. The person then takes a cold bath or shower to rinse the sweat and dirt from the skin.

***Right*** *A lamp provides some warmth and light in a snow igloo.*

Homes need to be built with care if they are to function properly and do the job they are built to do. A house in a cold place needs to be able to protect its occupants from the harsh elements outside. It is often thought of as a machine for living in. But a house is more than a machine. It is a personal, private place for a particular family. No two homes ever look the same inside. Individual homes are unique because people are different, with varying needs and ideas.

***Above*** *A sauna is both relaxing and cleansing. A person sits in a room filled with steam or dry heat and then takes a cold bath or shower.*

***Right*** *A fire in the center of a laavu tent is used for cooking by this traditional Lapp family.*

# Glossary

**airlock** A chamber between the outer air and an inner room
**caulking** Putty or plastic used to stop air leaks around windows and doors
**climate** The usual weather a place has over a very long period
**conserve** Save or preserve
**culture** The way of life shared by a group of people, including their language, arts, and beliefs
**double or triple glazing** Two or three layers of glass panes in a window
**draft** A current of air flowing in an enclosed space
**earth-sheltered house** A house built partly underground
**energy** the vigorous exertion of power
**fiberglass insulation** A material made of fine, matted glass fibers
**foundation** The base on which the walls of a house stand
**freezing point** The temperature at which water becomes solid: 32° F (0° C)
**igloo** The Inuit word for any house. This often refers to a dome-shaped building made of snow blocks.
**inaccessible** Unable to be reached
**industrial** Relating to work that makes or prepares something for sale
**insulate** Applying materials to block the flow of heat from a body or structure
**laavu** A tent in which the Lapp people live when herding reindeer
**lattice** A crisscross pattern of wood or bars
**nomad** A person with no permanent home who travels searching for food, work, or pastureland.
**permafrost** Ground that is frozen all the time, often to great depths
**prefabricated** Partly assembled before arriving at a building site
**research** Careful study or observation carried out to learn new facts
**shingle** Rectangular roof tile
**shutter** Moveable cover for the outside of a window, usually made of wood
**slate** A flat piece of split rock used as roofing material
**sod** A mat of soil, thick grass, and plant roots
**spiral** A coiled shape that winds around a central point
**surface area** The amount of exposed space on the outside of a a building
**temperature** The amount of heat in a place or thing
**thatched roof** A roof covered with reeds, straw, or leaves
**tropics** The area of the earth's surface near the equator
**tundra lands** Bare, cold areas of the Arctic where only grass, moss, and bushes grow
**wall cavity** A hollow space between the outer and inner layers of a wall
**whiteout** A thick snow cloud through which nothing can be seen
**yurt** A type of tent built by Mongolian nomads

# Books to read

*An Eskimo Family* by Bryan and Cherry Alexander (Lerner Publications, 1979)
*Antarctica* by Gardner Soule (Franklin Watts, 1985)
*Building A House* by Ken Robbins (Four Winds Press, 1984)
*Greenland: Island at the Top of the World* by Madelyn Klein Anderson (Dodd, Mead & Company, 1983)
*Homes and Cities* by Colin Moorcraft (Franklin Watts, 1982)
*Houses: Shelters from Prehistoric Times to Today* by Anne Siberell (Holt, Rinehart & Winston, 1979)

## Houses and Homes

| | |
|---|---|
| Building Homes | Homes in Space |
| Castles and Mansions | Homes in the Future |
| Homes in Cold Places | Homes on Water |
| Homes in Hot Places | Mobile Homes |

**Picture acknowledgements**

The author and publishers would like to thank the following for the illustrations in this book: Bryan and Cherry Alexander, pp. 4, 6, 8, 9, 11, 15 (bottom), 16 (both), 18, 20, 21 (bottom), 24, 26, 27 (top), 28, 29 (bottom); Chris Fairclough, p. 14; Hutchison Library, pp. 13 (both), 15 (top), 19 (bottom); Miriam Moss, p. 22; Society for Cultural Relations with the U.S.S.R., p. 25; John Wright, p. 21, (top); ZEFA, pp. 7, 19 (top), 23 (both), 27 (bottom), 29 (top), Bryan and Cherry Alexander, *cover.*

# Index

Numbers in **bold** refer to illustrations


Alaska, 5, **23**
Alps, 5
animals, 4, **4,** 8, 22
Antarctic, 4, 5, 6, **6,** 18-19, 23, 24, 26, **27**
apartment houses, **15,** 17, **17**
Arctic, 4, **4,** 5, **20,** 24, **24,** 26
Arctic trading post, **9**
attic insulation, **10,** 11
Austria, 5, 14
Canada, 5, 7, **9,** 17, 18, **18, 20,** 22, 24, **24**
central heating, 28
chalet, 14, **14**
double glazing, **10,** 11
earth-sheltered houses, 20
electricity, 9
Falkland Islands, 5
Faroe Islands, **11**
Finland, 5, **16,** 28
France, 14
Germany, 14
Greenland, 5, 22
Himalayan Mountains, 5, **23**
Huichol, 20
hunting, 22
Iceland, 5, 11
igloos, **8,** 11, 12, **12,** 18, 20, 26, **27, 28**
India, 5, **22**
insulation, 9, **10,** 11, 20, **20**
Inuit, 11, 12, **20,** 22, **23**
laavu tents, **16,** 17, **21, 29**
Lapp people, **16,** 17, 20, 22, **29**
log house, 16-17, **16,** 20
Mexico, 5, 20
nomads, 13, 17, 22
North Pole, 4
Norway, 5, **21**
permafrost, 7
Peru, 5
prefabricated houses, 17, **17**
Quechua Indians, **21**
research stations, 6, **6,** 18-19, 23, 24, 26
roofs, 11, **11,** 14, **15,** 17
saunas, 28, **29**
Scandinavia, 20, 28
shutters, 17
Siberia, 26, **26**
solar panels, 18, **19**
South America, 5, 20
South Pole, 4
Spitzbergen, 5
Sweden, 5, 18, 28
Switzerland, **5,** 14, **14, 15**
tents, 13, **13, 16,** 17, 20, **21,** 22
Tibet, 5
Tierra del Fuego, 20
triple glazing, 11
tundra, 4-5, 7
U.S.A., **7, 23**
U.S.S.R., 5, **15,** 17, **19,** 24, **25,** 26, **26**
wall cavity insulation, **10,** 11
wooden buildings, **7,** 11, 14, 22, 24, 26, **26**
yurt, 13, **13**